T0078039

COLLECTED POEMS

Thomas Orion

authorHOUSE

AuthorHouse™
1663 Liberty Drive
Bloomington, IN 47403
www.authorhouse.com
Phone: 833-262-8899

Published by AuthorHouse   10/07/2021

ISBN: 978-1-6655-4060-5 (sc)
ISBN: 978-1-6655-4059-9 (e)

Print information available on the last page.

This book is printed on acid-free paper.

Lillith Dear,
My Sign,

Are You in Order,
or do We Sign Caine.

We are the Nation,
We Sign the Stars.

I am Your Lucipher,
Your Laughter and Rain.

Sign Caine.
and Order.

Sign.

#1

I Wonder, in Awe
What we are, and What We Have.

This is an Instance of Love I Betray,
I Sleep and Awake, and I Beg and I Pray.

This is the Godhood, and I Say,
Betray this the Devil, and Say that I Nay.

This is Some, and a Wonder, is Near.
A New Bourne Baby, the Light of My Day.

Little Jesus, His Mom and a Crib.
Sign Jesus, the Lord, and a Sheep.
The Wonder is Near, and the Little Asleep.

Sign Jesus, this Christmas, Sign Laughter, Sign Joy.
Sign Motherhood, Father, Sign Mary, sign Roy.
The Royal, in Bethlehem, signed in a Night.
The Fatherhood, Jesus, Joseph and Joy.

This is a Testament, this is a Feast,
For Fatherhood, Saviour, Conquest and Meek.
For I am Believer, I am a Christ.
The Novel, the Light and Angelic Delight.
Sign Me a Christmas, and Sign it With Might.

In Order of this, the Sleeping, and Roy.
In this Do we Celebrate, Christmas with Joy.

#2

In this Order, I am Sign.
I Sign the Rain.

I Sign the Moon.
I Sign Order.

I sign You.
Order.

This is the Life.
This is Eternity.

This is a Laugh.
I sign Again.

Laugh.

#3

This Station, is Nice.
The Order is Sign.

I Sign the Station.
Order.

#4

Station Order.
This is Nice.

I Order.
Copy.

Id.

#5

These Times are Awefull.
We Sign Order.

I am an Adept.
Element.
Sign.

#6

Stanza
Order

Sign
Id

#7

Enumeration is Easy.
Thought is Hard.

My Computer is Drive.
Hard Drive.

Sign.

#8

All these Tokens,
are Mine.

One Left Standing,
and Blind.

I sign,
Order.

Mine.

#9

See these Orders, and Sign.
Wise Men Sage, and Kind.

One Order, Through, and Enough.
We are Sages, Aligned.

Court Order,
Notion.

Sign.

#10

These Orders Are the Same, I Remind.
the Court of a Dreamer, in Sign.

I Order these, a New.

And Long Forgotten, Intoxications,
Of a Stable Brew.

Salute.

#11

Salute Ideom.
Sign the Stars.

Sign with Mars,
and Mercury, my Friend.

I am Luna, and I Love,
My Master Above.

Sol Rex,
in Order.

Sign Word,
and Lord.

#12

These Evidences are my Fathom,
I Endure.

Sign these,
And Order.

Another Manure.
These Evidences,
Are,

The Notion of my Mind,
At Far.

#13

Sign Order,
sign my Life.

Do Bother,
City Life.

I am,
I Can.

I Order
Survival,

in the City.

#14

Nowhere in these Fathoms,
are alike.

The Dragon Signs,
Amidst a Wake.

I Sign these,
Orders,

And So.
The Mother of Whores,

Are Dint,
with Who.

Salutations.

#15

Amidst these Whores,
I Order.

Peace.

An Hope that the Lyre,
Will Play Something Greece.

In Order, we Sign.
The Whore and a Lute.

Put Whistle above, Your Flute.

16

No More Pain.
Again and Again.

Sign the Love, with a
Deamoness Dove.

We Sign Order,
and I am.

Sign Wonder,
and Learn.

Peace.

#17

In Order of this, I Sign,
the Heavenly Orders of Gunpowder,
Ashes and Pain.

This Outmost Enduire.
This Legacy of Eternity.

We Endure the Moon,
and the Stars.

But in Order,
Mars.

#18

There are these Orders, and we
Sign with the Presence of Maybe.

We are the Order, of Haught.
We Sign the Nomen, of Naught.

Sign this.

#19

This Nomen is Mine, I Order.
Sign this, and Be

Mine,
Forever.

#20

Status is Saught,
I Order.

Nomen is Wraught,
and Order.

Order,
Sign.

#21

These Instances, I Endure,
these are,

A Window, to the Night,
And Order.

Sign.

#22

Somesuch, Order.
And I Deign.

The Mother of Whores,
and Sign.

Copy Order,
and Hop,

These Signs,
Whop.

#23

Carpe Diem.
It Seems, like a Naught,

but I Saught,
this,

and Order,
Sign.

#24

These Instances,
that Maur.

I am these, and AUR.
We Sing, the Priesthood,
in Order,
and Notion.

LOVE, and SPIRIT,
Sign.

#25

These are My Days, and I Order,
the Lord, of Flies, that I
Wonder,

What is the World,
without Plies.

#26

In these Orders, we Sign.
I am Ordeals, Benign.

We are Saint,
and I am.

The Vain, of Said.

#27

These are Orders, and we Are,
the Notion of Corridors, that
Wine.

We Said,
and Say.

Thine.

#28

Station Op.
In these Desires.

We Come,
to Audent Admires.

We Sign.
Station.

#29

Station, Order, Sign.
We are Masters of the Mind.

We Live, Survive, and Deal.
A Station, Real.

We Sign.
We Serve.

- GOD -

How Odd.

#30

These Signs, is an Oddity.
When Quaint is Nothing, and
Ordeal, is a Pottery.

Sign Master, Sign GOD.
Sign Order, Sign LORD.

Master Order,
and Love.

Sign Borders, Sign Law.
Sign Elements, and Fire.

Water Admire.
Sign Air, and Earth.

Sign Women, Sign Birth.
Sign Christian, Sign Jehesua,
In Order, Sign Love.

And the Border.
We Are, and by Jove,

Sign Borders,
Sign the DOVE.

#31

Station Order,
sign Ordeal.

Copy.

#32

These Orders, are my Sign.
I Sage and Wonder, in the Rain.

Sophomore Treas, Injunction While.
The Standard Studio inconcile.

We are Masters, we are Sign.
But the Dozen and Drink the Wine.

#33

There are No Thing in the World,
Which is a Dozen Tribalds, Courted Courled.

These are Sanctions, these are Fire.
What we Sign and Admire.

Sign the Sire.

#34

We are the World, We Design.
We are Placent, we are Swine.

We Sign Notion,
We are Dead,

We Dispose the Origin,
We are Fed.

We Live.

#35

Sign the Cross, Order Wine.
Do the Circle, Feast Like Swine.

Copy Notion,
Order Mint.

Sign the Potion,
Copy Dint.

We are Notion, we Sign War.
We Dispose the Origin, in a Jar.

Copy These, Order Naught.
Caight in a Dance, Oblibion Haught.

Swine.

#36

These Orders, that we Entertain, are
A Nought in the Wheel of the Universe.

We Gain, Nought.
And We.

Sign Thought,
Whith a Thistle of Fern.

Sign Thought,
and Hern.

#37

Orders Are, the Nought of Religion,
but, Order is that Station of GOD.

So,
in Order of this,
I Sign.

Ordeal.

#38

This Station, is,
A Nullabore Plains,

in Australia,
she Is.

#39

Once a Vengeance, is,
a Nothing, in Tears.

So Sign,
Sears.

#40

This is Lot, I am Fourty.
So I Sign my Worthy.

We are Sign,
I am Notion.

Drink the Beer,
that Vigilant Potion.

#41

In Order of this, we Say
Thou Mayest Conquor the Light
but Pray.

That a Mantis, is Green and the
Sky, is Blue.

Find an Order, and Choose a Hue.

42

Do, thee
Night.

Order Sign,
and Plight.

43

Order Cosmos, Order Sign.
Sign the Vilest Dreams, of Order
and Attain.

Sign these,
Sign the LORD.

Copy Office,
Order HOB.

Copy,
Nought.

#44

These instances, that I Adore,
these Signs, are Above.

I Sign the Lion.
I Sign the Cat.

Order Above.
Sign that.

#45

These Nouns, are at All.
They are the Sound, of the Eternal.

Sign Eternity, Sign GOD.
Station Divinity, Station NOD.

#46

Novel Signs.
Of Ordained.

This Priest a Saint.

We Welcome, the Order, of Lust.
And Sign a Mason, Just.

So be it, this Trigon.
And Copy, the Soldier, Done.

#47

Station These, Order that.
Sign a Novel, Order of TAT.

This is IT, the Novel, and in Sign
a Bowel of Abdomen.

Just Sign DID.

#48

These are the Signs, of a State.
Sign this Colonne of Might.

I am Order, this is It.
No Wonder, Sign Bid.

Hurray.

#49

These Signs, are in Order.
I Say.

No Wonder.
Sign.

#50

No Order is Alone.
These Signs, Above.

Sign the Covet of a Dove.
And Done.

#51

These Orders, that I Give.
These Nouns, in which I Believe.

There Are Sage.
There is Noun.

None Found.

#52

Order these.
Sign this.

Do this.
With Ease.

Sign.

##

Printed in the United States
by Baker & Taylor Publisher Services